# » Sonnets of Love & Death

» Jean de Sponde

# Sonnets *of* Love *&* Death

A BILINGUAL EDITION

TRANSLATED FROM THE FRENCH

BY DAVID R. SLAVITT

NORTHWESTERN UNIVERSITY PRESS

EVANSTON, ILLINOIS

Northwestern University Press
Evanston, Illinois 60208-4210

Printed in the United States of America

10 9 8 7 6 5 4 3 2 1

ISBN 0-8101-1840-8

**Library of Congress Cataloging-in-Publication Data**

Sponde, Jean de, 1557–1595.

    [D'amour et de mort. English & French]

    Sonnets of love and death / Jean de Sponde ; translated from the French
by David R. Slavitt.—Bilingual ed.

        p.   cm.

    ISBN 0-8101-1840-8

    1. Sonnets, French—Translations into English. 2. Sonnets, French.
I. Slavitt, David R., 1935– II. Title.
PQ1705.S7 A275 2001
841'.3—dc21                                 2001001090

Sonnets X, XI, and XII of "Sonnets on Death" appeared in *TriQuarterly* 106 (fall 1999).

For Tatiana

# » Contents

Translator's Preface   ix

*Sonnets d'amour*
Sonnets on Love        3

*Sonnets de la mort*
Sonnets on Death       57

Bibliographic Note     83

# » Translator's Preface

Jean de Sponde (1557–95) was a humanist, a translator, a jurist, a polemicist, and an alchemist as well as a poet. He was born in the Basque country into a family that was probably Spanish in origin. He became an excellent Hellenist, and Chapman used his edition of Homer. He began as a Calvinist but converted to Catholicism in 1593 (after a year of imprisonment). He retired to Bordeaux, where he died in 1595 and was buried in the cathedral of Saint André.

Sponde offers a fascinating counterfactual in literary history, for his work, which is very much like that of Sir Philip Sidney or John Donne, suggests the direction that French poetry might have taken had it not been for the influence of François de Malherbe and of the Pléiade, who, during the tumultuous time of the Valois kings, set a pattern of—and a taste for—the classical poise and harmony that has informed French poetry and civilization ever since. His sonnets contain and constrain, although just barely, a mannerist restlessness, and their fascination is in the tension between their stylistic and philosophical polarities. He has been compared with Bronzino and Parmigianino in the fine arts and Gesualdo and Carissimi in music. His work that, for centuries, struck the French as mannerist seems to the Anglophone reader immediately congenial and even eerily familiar.

It was only in the twentieth century and with the changes in taste that were influenced by post-Romantic poetry—particularly that of Baudelaire and Mallarmé—that the French began to reconsider the work of Sponde. And it may well have been that this belated rekindling of their interest was occasioned by a British critic, Alan Boase, who drew attention to him in an article in 1930 in T. S. Eliot's *The Criterion*. In the second half of the twentieth century, Sponde's stock was high among the French, and at French-language scholarly meetings throughout the world the quality of his poems was at last getting the attention his work so clearly merits.

What attracted my attention to Sponde is the intimacy of the voice. These poems probably were not meant for publication or for any wide public at all but rather were private productions. They are personal confrontations with the great questions, and they are as technically dazzling as they are spiritually profound. My aim in this translation of Sponde's *D'amour et de la mort* was not only to make clear what the poems were in their time and place but, in a contemporary English rendering, to show what endures as eternal and universal in the struggle of an intelligent and passionate man with the anguishing questions of love and faith.

» Sonnets of Love & Death

*Sonnets d'amour*

Sonnets on Love

Si c'est dessus les eaux que la terre est pressée,
Comment se soutient-elle encor si fermement?
Et si c'est sur les vents qu'elle a son fondement,
Qui la peut conserver sans être renversée?

Ces justes contrepoids qui nous l'ont balancée,
Ne penchant-ils jamais d'un divers branlement?
Et qui nous fait solide ainsi cet Elément,
Qui trouve autour de lui l'inconstance amassée?

Il est ainsi: ce corps se va tout soulevant
Sana jamais s'ébranler parmi l'onde et le vent.
Miracle nonpareil! si mon amour extrême,

Voyant ces maux coulants, soufflants de tous cotés,
Ne trouvait tous les jours par exemple de même
Sa constance au milieu de ces légèretés.

Beneath the weight of the sea's incessant caress,
the earth somehow holds firm. How is this so?
Or think of the tousling winds that to and fro
rock the world's foundation. Nevertheless,

it does not fly apart. Somehow these two
different distractions cancel each other, maintain
a balance that's all the greater for their strain,
and produce an illusion of steadiness we think true.

The body works this way: the sudden gales
assault and threaten us all, females and males,
who manage some show of decorous behavior,

and if we appear to be constant in our affections
it may be because of tugs in different directions,
inconstancy serving thus as fidelity's savior.

Quand je vois les efforts de ce grand Alexandre,
D'un César dont le sein comblé de passions
Embrase tout du feu de ses ambitions,
Et n'en laisse après soi mémoire qu'en la cendre:

Quand je vois que leur gloire est seulement de rendre
(Après l'orage enflé de tant d'afflictions)
Calmes dessous leurs lois toutes les nations
Qui voient le Soleil et monter et descendre:

Encor que j'ai de quoi m'enorgueillir comme eux,
Que mes lauriers ne soient de leurs lauriers honteux,
Je les condamne tous et ne les puis défendre:

Ma belle, c'est vers toi que tournent mes esprits,
Ces tyrans-là faisaient leur triomphe de prendre,
Et je triompherai de ce que tu m'as pris.

I think of the great Alexander and what he won
or Caesar whose breast was burning with that same
appetite for conquest, power, and fame. . . .
But those fires die to ashes when they are done.

Such triumphs never endure. An army's hard
campaign in a distant province may put down
another army; they'll occupy a town
under a treaty that time will disregard.

I can take pride as much as either of them
and wear as impressive a laurel diadem
as ever a tyrant won by martial art.

They captured distant territories, true,
but I have lost the world and my soul to you
and in my surrender triumph in my heart.

Qui serait dans les cieux, et baisserait sa vue
Sur le large pourpis de ce sec élément
Il ne croirait le Tout rien qu'un point seulement,
Un point encor caché du voile d'une nue:

Mais s'il contemple après cette courtine bleue,
Ce cercle de cristal, ce doré firmament,
Il juge que son tour est grand infiniment,
Et que cette grandeur nous est toute inconnue.

Ainsi de ce grand ciel, où l'amour m'a guidé,
De ce grand ciel d'Amour où mon oeil est bandé,
Si je relâche un peu la pointe aiguë au reste,

Au reste des amours, je vois sous une nuit
Le monde d'Epicure en atomes réduit,
Leur amour tout de terre, et le mien tout céleste.

Imagine yourself in the heavens, floating high
and looking down through the clouds, peering at what
we call the wide world—this little dot
in the firmament, a mere mote in the eye.

From here, in reverse, we gaze at crystal spheres
and further golden realms that stretch away
in infinite unimaginable array.
What we know of love we infer from what appears

in this perspective. Whirling bits of dust
are everywhere: the atoms in their lust
for one another dance the same quadrille

the planets perform, and the distant galaxies.
The mind of matter is manifest in these
displays of desire, energy, and will.

En vain mille beautés à mes yeux se présentent,
Mes yeux leur sont ouverts et mon courage clos,
Une seule beauté s'enflamme dans mes os
Et mes os de ce feu seulement se contentent:

Les rigueurs de ma vie et du temps, qui m'absentent
Du bien-heureux séjour où loge mon repos,
Altèrent moins mon âme, encor que mon propos
Et mes discrets désirs jamais ne se repentent.

Chatouilleuses beautés, vous domptez doucement
Tous ces esprits flottants, qui souillent aisément
Des absentes amours la chaste souvenance:

Mais pour tous vos efforts je demeure indompté:
Ainsi je veux servir d'un patron de constance,
Comme ma belle fleur d'un patron de beauté.

A thousand beauties pass before my eyes
in a vain parade, for in my bones the fire
that burns is for one only. My desire
is for her beauty alone that satisfies

my craving. Far away from her I languish,
ignoring such other hardships as heat or cold
which are nothing at all to me, who am consoled
by grief and am anesthetized by anguish.

You touchy ticklish beauties here at court
may bedazzle some whose attention span is short,
but I am blind and deaf to all your flirting.

I do not propose myself as a model of
the cavalier who enters the lists of love;
for doctors, I am a case of constant hurting.

Je meurs, et les soucis, qui sortent du martyre
Que me donne l'absence, et les jours, et les nuits
Font tant qu'à tous moments je ne sais que je suis,
Si j'empire du tout ou bien si je respire.

Un chagrin survenant mille chagrins m'attire,
En me cuidant aider moi-même je me nuis;
L'infini mouvement de mes roulants ennuis
M'emporte, et je le sens, mais je ne le puis dire.

Je suis cet Actéon de ses chiens déchiré!
Et l'éclat de mon âme est si bien altéré
Qu'elle, qui devrait me faire vivre, me tue:

Deux Déesses nous ont tramé tout notre sort,
Mais pour divers sujets nous trouvons même mort,
Moi de ne la voir point, et lui de l'avoir vue.

» » » V

I die with the burdens of martyrdom: your distance
is torture, moment by moment, that I endure
in utter despair for which there is no cure,
and my own heart's and lungs' absurd persistence

mocks me, protracts my pain, and turns my mind
to fantasies of self-destruction and peace—
but the distance between us then would only increase.
I am Actaeon; his pack of hounds are combined

in this one body that tears at its master in rage.
And she to whom I pray does not assuage
my sufferings. When I am close to her I ache,

but far away I also suffer: I burn
or else, in cold and darkness, freeze. I yearn
for her, and either way my heart must break.

Mon Dieu, que je voudrais que ma main fût oisive,
Que ma bouche et mes yeux reprissent leur devoir!
Ecrire est peu: c'est plus de parler et de voir,
De ces deux oeuvres l'une est morte et l'autre vive.

Quelque beau trait d'amour que notre main écrive,
Ce sont témoins muets qui n'ont pas le pouvoir
Ni le semblable poids, que l'oeil pourrait avoir
Et de nos vives voix la vertu plus naïve.

Mais quoi? n'étaient encor ces faibles étançons
Et ces fruits mi-rongés dont nous le nourrissons
L'Amour mourrait de faim et cherrait en ruine:

Ecrivons, attendant de plus fermes plaisirs,
Et si le temps domine encor sur nos désirs,
Faisons que sur le temps la constance domine.

We take our lives in our hands, they say. I fear
my own is too much there as I scrawl on a sheet
of paper words my mouth should be saying, the sweet
nothings I ought to be whispering into her ear.

Words on a page are dead unlike those that fly
in the air, alive and potent. The human voice,
happy or sad, seems the much better choice
than ink that glistens but then turns dull and dry.

And yet these representations endure, this token
the hand can hold, as the ear cannot with spoken
endearments that fall through memory's coarse sieve.

Over time our desires and pleasures fade:
it is nature's law, which we may yet evade
by acting as if our love might forever live.

Si j'avais comme vous, mignardes colombelles,
Des plumages si beaux sur mon corps attachés,
On aurait beau tenir mes esprits empêchés
De l'indomptable fer de cent châines nouvelles:

Sur les ailes du vent je guiderais mes ailes,
J'irais jusqu'au séjour où mes biens sont cachés:
Ainsi voyant de moi ces ennuis arrachés,
Je ne sentirais plus ces absences cruelles.

Colombelles hélas! que j'ai bien souhaité
Que mon corps vous semblât autant d'agilité
Que mon âme d'amour à votre âme ressemble!

Mais quoi? Je la souhaite et me trompe d'autant.
Ferais-je bien voler un amour si constant
D'un monde tout rempli de vos ailes ensemble?

If I were decked out in feathers the way you are,
would I not put them to use, perhaps to defy
gravity's law, flap my arms, and fly
on the winds of improbability, high and far,

as if in a children's story, to find the remote
dwelling place of my guardian spirit? She
might grant my wish and allow me always to be
beside you, to admire, adore, and dote.

But you are the one who sports those wings of the dove
that suggest those flights your soul is capable of,
way beyond mine, which is why I love you so.

Leaden, rooted to earth, I envy you
even as I admire, but part of me too
takes off, soars, and leaves this poor husk below.

Ce trésor que j'ai pris avec tant de peine
Je le veux avec peine encore conserver
Tardif à reposer, prompt à me relever,
Et tant veiller qu'en fin on ne me le surprenne.

Encor que de mes yeux la garde plus certaine
Auprès de son séjour ne se puisse trouver,
Et qu'il me peut encor en l'absence arriver
Qu'un autre plus prochain me l'empoigne et l'emmène.

Je ne veux pas pourtant me travailler ainsi,
Ta seule foi m'assure et m'ôte le souci:
Et ne changera point pourvu que je ne change.

Il faut tenir bon oeil et bon pied dur ce point:
A gagner un beau bien on gagne une louange.
Main on en gagne mille à ne le perdre point.

## »»» VIII

Late to bed and early to rise, alert,
I guard the treasure I won at such great price
and pay for again in the pains I take. My eyes
are never closed. I am touchy, jealous, hurt.

My loving gaze is on every face but hers:
I watch for smiles and gestures of assent
until I hate myself, despair, repent,
and resolve to trust in her—but that is worse,

for then I doubt myself. What I intend
is not yet what I am, who would defend
what I have won. And envy fills me again

of what I should like to be: suave, self-assured,
able to enjoy what I've secured,
and, when my prayers are answered, say Amen.

Si tant de maux passés ne m'ont acquis ce bien,
Que vous croyez au moins que je vous suis fidèle,
Ou si vous le croyez, qu'à la moindre querelle
Vous me fassiez semblant de n'en plus croire rien.

Belle, pour qui je meurs, belle, pensez-vous bien
Que je ne sente point cette injure cruelle?
Plus sanglante beaucoup que la peine éternelle,
Où malgré tout le monde encor je me retiens.

Il est vrai toutefois, vos beautés infinies,
Quand je vivrais encor cent mille et mille vies,
Ne se pourraient jamais servir si dignement.

Que je ne fusse en reste à leur valeur parfaite:
Mais croyez-le ou non, la preuve est toute faite
Qu'au prix de moi, l'Amour aime imparfaitement.

If, after all those evil days, I arrive
at a happiness like this, can you suppose
I'd risk what I have found with you? God knows
I'd have to be the stupidest man alive

to be unfaithful. Do I seem a fool to you?
For you to credit slanders villains tell
distresses me more than any vision of hell,
in fear of which I swear that I am true.

I say my ardor, like your beauty, is
infinite and absolute. In this
a thousand lifetimes could not find defect.

The very idea of love must look to us
to learn its own perfection, envious
of the miracle we have made and must protect.

Je ne bouge non plus qu'un écueil dedans l'onde
Qui fait fort à l'orage et le fait reculer.
Il me trouve affermi, qui cherche à m'ébranler,
Dussé-je voir branler contre moi tout le monde.

Chacun qui voit combien tous les jours je me fonde
Sue ce constant dessein, se mêle d'en parler,
Trouble la terre et l'air afin de me troubler,
Et ne pouvant rien plus, pour le moins il en gronde.

Mais je n'écoute point (que pour le mépriser)
Ce propos enchanteur qui tend à m'abuser
Et me ravir le bien que leur rage m'envie.

Laissons, laissons-les dire, un seul mot me suffit:
Qu'en la guerre d'amour une âme bien nourrie
Emporte tout l'honneur emportant le profit.

## »»» X

Stolid as some offshore reef the storm
churns waves over to seethe and then fall back,
I am unmoved and, stronger for each attack,
I wait for the next conspiracy to form.

My enemies, dismayed, discuss my calm
their agitation cannot ruffle. The more
they do, the less effect it has. In war
and love, the indifferent triumph. And I am.

What I have learned from strife, I put to use
in the lists of love, where the white flags of truce
and of surrender look much the same. The sweet

spoils are there for the taking, and honor requires
a boldness that never wavers and never tires
until it has wrested its prize on that snowy sheet.

Tous mes propos jadis ne vous faisaient instance
Que de l'ardent amour dont j'étais embrasé:
Mais depuis que votre oeil sur moi s'est apaisé
Je ne puis vous parler rien que de ma constance.

L'Amour même de qui j'éprouve l'assistance,
Qui sait combien l'esprit de l'homme est fort aisé
D'aller aux changements, se tient comme abusé
Voyant qu'en vous aimant j'aime sans repentance.

Il s'en remontre assez qui brûlent vivement,
Mais la fin de leur feu, qui se va consommant,
N'est qu'un brin de fumée et qu'un morceau de cendre.

Je laisse ces amants croupir en leurs humeurs
Et me tiens pour content, s'il vous plaît de comprendre
Que mon feu ne saurait mourir si je ne meurs.

Before, my protestations of love, though fervent,
were mere displays of generic desire. Now
that your eyes have met my gaze and you allow
my devotion, I speak differently, your servant,

in love no more with love itself but you,
and yet I must acknowledge that ideal
mistress whom I have deserted for the real
woman and sing those praises that are her due.

Her cavaliers consume themselves and burn
brightly for a time until they turn
to wisps of smoke and piles of ashes. But I,

nourished by your changing moods, can find
refreshment every moment and am refined
in a fire that will rage until I die.

Mon coeur, ne te rends point à ces ennuis d'absence,
Et quelque forts qu'ils soient, sois encore plus fort;
Quand même tu serais sur le point de la mort,
Mon coeur, ne te rends point et reprends ta puissance.

Que si tant de combats te donnent connaissance
Que tu n'es pas toujours pour rompre leur effort,
Garde-toi de tomber dans un tel déconfort
Que ton amour jamais y perde son essence.

Puis que tous tes soupirs sont ainsi retardés,
Laisse, laisse courir ces torrents débordés,
Et monte sur les rocs de ce mont de constance:

Ainsi dessus les monts ce sage chef Romain
Différa ses combats du jour au lendemain,
Se moqua d'Hannibal, rompant sa violence.

» » » XII

Worse than any battle, this ennui
in which I find myself threatens to break
my heart, my spirit—I resolve to make
ready to be besieged. Not gallantry

but patience is required, and faith. The hours
drag on and my desire becomes my foe.
Deaf to all reason, rebellious, full of woe,
my heart resists my intellectual powers.

Quintus Fabius Maximus showed that the way
to win is not by fighting but delay.
Thus did the famous Cunctator survive,

and Hannibal's force, frustrated, was defied.
Skirmish like him and keep yourself occupied
and you may yet come out of this alive.

Tu disais, Archimède, ainsi qu'on nous rapporte,
Qu'on te donnât un point pour bien te soutenir,
Tu branlerais le monde, et le ferais venir,
Comme un faix plus léger de lieu en lieu s'emporte.

Puis que ton arc si beau, ta main était si forte,
Si tu pouvais encor au monde revenir,
Dans l'amour que mon coeur s'efforce à retenir
Tu trouverais ton point peut être en quelque sorte.

Pourrait-on voir jamais plus de solidité
Qu'en ce qui branle moins plus il est agité
Et prend son assurance en l'inconstance même:

Il est sûr, Archimède, et je n'en doute point:
Pour branler tout le Monde et s'assurer d'un point,
Il te fallait aimer aussi ferme que j'aime.

"Give me a place to stand," Archimedes said,
"and I can move the world." Paradoxical, clever,
his remark which first explained the use of the lever
was an academic joke. But if that dead

sage could return to life, he would find a clear
demonstration of his idea, which is not
pure theory after all. That putative spot
exists in the love I feel for you, my dear.

What could be more immovable or stronger?
What becomes more and more secure, the longer
it is battered by inconstancy and the stress

we find in our lives? Here is that fine fixed point
from which to move a world that is out of joint,
as he could have done, had he known a love like this.

Quand le vaillant Hector, le grand rempart de Troie,
Sortit tout enflammé, sur les nefs des Grégeois,
Et qu'Achille charmait d'une plaintive voix
Son oisive douleur, sa vengeance de joie;

Comme quand le Soleil dedans l'onde flamboie,
L'onde des rais tremblants repousse dans les toits;
La Grèce tout ainsi flottante cette fois
Eût peur d'être à la fin la proie de sa proie.

Un seul bouclier d'Ajax se trouvant le plus fort
Soutint cette fureur et dompta cet effort.
J'eusse perdu de même en cette horrible absence,

Mon amour, assailli d'une armée d'ennuis,
Dans le travail des jours, dans la langueur des nuits;
Si je ne l'eusse armé d'un bouclier de constance.

When valiant Hector comes down from the wall of Troy
ablaze with rage at the black ships of the Greeks;
when Achilles keeps to his tent and sulks and speaks
or sings the complaints that now are his only joy;

when the sun with its rays seems to assault the waves
that return the fire in a dazzling enfilade;
and the Greeks in their camp they have pitched on the
    beach are afraid
that their cause is lost; then mighty Ajax braves

this combination of dangers with his shield
that blazes bright in the sunshine and will not yield.
So I defy your absence, its alarms,

my fantasies, and the gnawing doubts that loom
large in the darkened corners of my room,
and remember our love, that blazon of my arms.

Cette brave Carthage, un des honneurs du monde
Et la longue terreur de l'empire Romain,
Qui donna tant de peine à son coeur, à sa main,
Pour se faire première, et Rome la seconde:

Après avoir dompté presque la terre et l'onde,
Et porté dans le ciel tout l'orgueil de son sein,
Eprouva mais trop tard, qu'un superbe dessein
Fondé dessus le vent, il faut en fin qu'il fonde.

Cette insolente-là! la pompe qu'elle aima!
Le brasier dévorant du feu la consuma:
Que je me ris au lieu, Carthage, de te plaindre.

Ton feu dura vingt jours, et brûla pour si peu.
Hélas! que dirais-tu si tu voyais qu'un feu
Me brûle si longtemps sans qu'il se puisse éteindre?

Consider Carthage, that rival of Rome: its pride,
boundless and overweening, turned to hate,
and it wanted to rule the world, the single great
power that had no equal by its side.

Therefore, it took up arms. We all know how
it triumphed over much of the earth until
it learned that strength is not the same as will
and came to utter ruin, so that now

we say its name in pity or even scorn.
For three weeks Romans watched its buildings burn
and then they sowed its fields with salt. But I

have burned even longer than that in a defeat
as absolute. I suffer my fires' heat
that rages without end, but I do not die.

Je prends exemple en toi, courageuse Numance,
L'un des grands fléaux de Rome, et comme toi je veux,
Pratiquant la valeur, apprendre à nos neveux
Qu'il faut vaincre en l'assaut, mourir en la défense.

Durant tes quatorze ans, l'insolente arrogance
De tes longs ennemis, du bon heur dépourvus,
Contre tant de vertu s'arrachait les cheveux
Et s'arrachait plus fort encore l'espérance:

Enfin on n'eut moyen propre à te surmonter
Que te laisser toi-même à toi-même dompter,
Et toi tu ne laissas que tes murs et ta cendre:

Ainsi tous ces ennuis dont je vaincs les efforts,
S'ils se trouvent enfin plus rusés que plus forts,
J'aime mieux comme toi mourir que de me rendre.

Numantia, I take my example from you,
the scourge of Rome, valiant, albeit doomed,
and look to your brave heroes who all assumed
that victory and death were the only two

choices. For fourteen years you carried on
in the struggle against a stronger foe who tore
their hair in their frustration at a war
they could not finish and you nearly won.

Then Scipio besieged you and it was clear
that every hope was gone and the end was near,
your soldiers killed themselves and burned their town

rather than surrender. Likewise, I
will not resign the battle: I'd rather die,
with honor, true to myself as I go down.

Je sens dedans mon âme une guerre civile,
D'un parti ma raison, mes sens d'autre parti,
Dont le brûlant discord ne peut être amorti,
Tant chacun son tranchant l'un contre l'autre affile.

Mais mes sens sont armés d'un verre si fragile
Que si le coeur bientôt ne s'en est départi,
Tout l'heur vers ma raison se verra converti,
Comme au parti plus fort, plus juste et plus utile.

Mes sens veulent ployer sous ce pesant fardeau
Des ardeurs que me donne un éloigné flambeau;
Au rebours, la raison me renforce au martyre.

Faisons comme dans Rome, à ce peuple mutin
De mes sens inconstants, arrachons-les enfin!
Et que notre raison y plante son Empire.

I feel in my soul a civil war—the most
uncivil war there is. On one side, reason
asserts its rule and accuses the senses of treason.
All hopes of peace and compromise seem lost.

My senses, fragile and hyperactive, assault
and threaten to break my heart, where reason's sway
has been my settled preference until today,
when all is in turmoil. It is not my fault,

for it is against my will that ardor has lit
its fires for that martyrdom my wit
does not at all desire or approve.

I call on the will's militia to restore
order and put this riot down before
my reason flees and abdicates to love.

Ne vous étonnez point si mon esprit, qui passe
De travail en travail par tant de mouvements,
Depuis qu'il est banni dans ces éloignements,
Tout agile qu'il est, ne change point de place.

Ce que vous en voyez, quelque chose qu'il fasse,
Il s'est planté si bien sur si bons fondements,
Qu'il ne voudrait jamais souffrir de changements,
Si ce n'est que le feu se peut changer de place.

Ces deux contraires sont en moi seul arrêtés,
Les faibles mouvements, les dures fermetés:
Mais voulez-vous avoir plus claire connaissance

Que mon espoir se meurt et ne change point?
Il tournoie à l'entour du point de la constance
Comme le Ciel tournoie à l'entour de son point.

My mind appears to wander? Perhaps, and yet
though subject gives way to subject and I can seem
distracted, undone by love, and I sometimes dream,
there is a fixity nonetheless: I am set

secure on my foundation. As, in the sky,
the constellations move but then return
according to their schedule which we learn
by constant observation, so in my

intellectual apparatus, weak
and strong are mixed together where they seek
a balance of hope and desperation. See

the twinkling stars, the planets, and the showers
of meteors that display the singular powers
of the firmament as it turns on its axle-tree.

Je contemplais un jour le dormant de ce fleuve
Que traîne lentement les ondes dans la mer,
Sans que les Aquilons le fassent écumer
Ni bondir, ravageur, sur les bords qu'il abreuve.

Et contemplant le cours de ces maux que j'épreuve,
Ce fleuve, dis-je alors, ne sait que c'est d'aimer;
Si quelque flamme eût pu ses glaces allumer,
Il trouverait l'amour ainsi que je le trouve;

S'il le sentait si bien, il aurait plus de flots.
L'Amour est de la peine et non point du repos,
Mais cette peine enfin est du repos suivie,

Si son esprit constant la défend du trépas:
Mais qui meurt en la peine il ne mérite pas
Que le repos jamais lui redonne la vie.

From the bank, I watched the placid river flow
inexorably toward the sea. The day
was calm; no breezes whipped up waves to spray
the shore. It went about its business, slow

and deliberate, unaffected by emotion—
love, for instance, from whose consuming flame
it is immune, or anger, or pride, or shame—
disturbing its stately progress toward the ocean.

Surely, not love. Such painlessness, such peace,
we sometimes yearn for, dreaming of a release
other than what death promises, but we keep

our minds fixed on our goal, the hopes that give
meaning to lives we otherwise should live
incompletely, as if in a dreamless sleep.

Les Toscans bataillaient, donnant droit dedans Rome,
Les armes à la main, la fureur sur le front,
Quand on voit un Horace avancer sur le pont
Et d'un coup arrêter tant d'hommes par un homme.

Après un long combat, ce brave qu'on renomme
Vaincu, non de valeur mais du grand nombre, rompt
De sa main le passage, et s'élance d'un bond
Dans le Tibre, se sauve, et sauve tout en somme.

Mon amour n'est pas moindre, et quoi qu'il soit surpris
De la foule d'ennuis qui troublent mes esprits,
Il fait ferme et se bat avec tant de constance

Que près des coups il est éloigné du danger;
Et s'il se doit enfin dans ses larmes plonger,
Le dernier désespoir sera son espérance.

» » » XX

The Tuscans are on the march toward Rome, with shield
and sword agleam, and their eyes, as the sunlight dances
in fury. . . . And then Horatio advances
and fights them one by one. He does not yield

but stands fast on the bridge, outnumbered though
never outfought. We think that he has died,
but he's still there; he's climbing over the side;
he escapes, jumping into the Tiber below.

My love is like him—beset with manifold
troubles—yet will it stand firm and hold
in monomaniacal valor its difficult post.

But if, at the last, it gives way to despair
and plunges into the river, a solace there
awaits—my knowledge that no more can be lost.

Non, je ne cache point une flamme si belle,
Je veux, je veux avoir tout le monde à témoin,
Et ceux qui sont plus près, et ceux qui sont plus loin;
Dites, est-il au monde un amant plus fidèle?

Ces secrètes humeurs (qu'hypocrites j'appelle)
Blâment secrètement à l'oreille en un coin
La peine que je prends d'en prendre tant de soin,
Tandis que chacun d'eux ses propres sens recèle.

Ainsi nous différons, qui leurs coeurs sont couverts
Et que le mien fait voir ses mouvements ouverts;
Ils ont raison, leurs sens sont bien dignes de honte:

Mais je ne puis rougir d'aimer si dignement,
Et plus mon bel amour tous leurs amours surmonte:
Il me le faut encor aimer plus constamment.

No, sir, the torch I carry is too bright,
too beautiful to conceal. I want to show
the world its light so everyone may know
what love looks like when it is true and right.

There is no excuse for shyness. Should I lurk
in corners to ogle, eavesdrop, even stalk . . . ?
That would be shameful. Better far to talk
openly of my passion. Who will smirk

or giggle? Let her see my savoir faire
as I ignore them, and let them blush who dare
make light of such a passion as mine. I'll never

think of any but her, who may believe
that I am hers—my heart is on my sleeve—
and that this flame will burn for her forever.

On dit que dans le ciel, les diverses images
Des astres l'un à l'autre ensemble rapportés
Engendrent ici bas tant de diversités
Et tantôt de profits et tantôt de dommages:

Tous les états leur font à leur tour leurs hommages,
L'un baisse, l'autre hausse: et tant de dignités
Ont en maintes façons certains points imités
Qui leur font et laisser et perdre leurs visages.

Mon amour sûr se trouve exempt de ces rigueurs,
Si ce n'est pour accroître encore ses vigueurs,
Mais non pas pour jamais d'un seul moment descendre.

Non pas s'il me fallait descendre dans la mort!
En somme il est (s'il faut par le ciel le comprendre)
Ferme ni plus ni moins que l'étoile du Nord.

Those figures the stars make in the zodiac
that spin in the sky occasion here on earth
desolation for one and, for another, mirth,
but awe from each of us who note their track

and attempt to fathom the secrets of Fortune's wheel
from what they figure, as we consider fate,
talent, and effort and try to allocate
their influences, and even to reveal

the obscurities of the future. But my love
can neither grow nor diminish. The stars above
are nothing then to me. Their cycles are

as irrelevant as an astrological chart.
I take my bearings rather from my heart:
its steadiness is that of the polar star.

Il est vrai, mon amour était sujet au change,
Avant que j'eusse appris d'aimer solidement,
Mais si je n'eusse vu cet astre consumant,
Je n'aurais point encor acquis cette louange.

Ores je vois combien c'est une humeur étrange
De vivre, mais mourir, parmi le changement,
Et que l'amour lui-même en gronde tellement
Qu'il est certain qu'enfin, quoiqu'il tarde, il s'en venge.

Si tu prends un chemin après tant de détours,
Un bord après l'orage, et puis reprends ton cours,
En l'orage, aux détours, s'il survient le naufrage

Ou l'erreur, on dira que tu l'as mérité.
Si l'amour n'est point feint, il aura le courage
De ne changer non plus que fait la vérité.

It's true, my love was once subject to change
before it found its proper object, that steady
star by which I steer. I had made ready
but wandered, lost and desperate, among the strange

vicissitudes of life on odd detours,
frightening then but entertaining now
as all past troubles are. I remember how
I staggered from one to another of my amours. . . .

But having seen the light and found the way
on which to set my feet, I will not stray,
lose heart, or faith, or courage. In my youth

I was beguiled, deluded, and prone to error,
a little boy before a distorting mirror.
I am wiser now and in love with her and truth.

Mon Soleil, qui brillez de vos yeux dans mes yeux,
Et pour trop de clarté leur ôtez la lumière,
Je ne vois rien que vous, et mon âme est si fière
Qu'elle ne daigne plus aimer que dans les cieux.

Tout autre amour me semble un enfer furieux,
Plein d'horreur et de mort, dont m'enfuyant arrière
J'en laisse franchement plus franche la carrière
A ceux qui font plus mal et pensent faire mieux.

Le plaisir, volontiers, est de l'amour l'amorce,
Mais outre encor je sens quelque plus vive force
Qui me ferait aimer malgré moi ce Soleil:

Cette force est en vous dont la beauté puissante,
La beauté sans pareille, encor qu'elle s'absente,
Attire cet amant, cet amant sans pareil.

You are my sun: your rays dazzle my eyes
and blind me to all else in the world. The whole
universe is shrunk to that point my soul
yearns for as it does for paradise.

All other loves are emptiness and gloom,
death's grand guignol, or hell's horrors I flee.
Let other lost souls, thinking they are free,
languish there in the dankness of the tomb.

Love sets such bait of pleasures in the night
to catch small scurrying creatures that the light
of your bright sun reveals as loathsomeness.

They are untrue to beauty and its power,
distracted if it be absent for an hour.
Blind to all that, my faith is effortless.

## XXV

Contemplez hardiment tous ceux qui font coutume
De se sacrifier à l'autel des beautés,
Vous verrez que le vent de leurs légèretés
Leur éteint le brasier aussitôt qu'il l'allume.

Mais moi, qui si longtemps à vos yeux me consume,
Je ne consume point pourtant mes fermetés,
Et d'autant plus avant au feu vous me mettez,
Plus l'or de mon amour à durer s'accoutume.

Pour vous, belle, le tout de ce Tout ne m'est rien,
Ces biens sont pauvretés au regard de ce Bien,
Et vous servir tant plus que mille et mille empires.

S'en trouve qui voudra vivement offensé,
Pour moi j'aimerais mieux mourir en vos martyres,
Que vivre au pus grand heur qui puisse être pensé.

## »»» XXV

Consider those whose custom it is to pray
at beauty's altar, where they make sacrifice,
lighting their votive candles that, in a trice,
a puff of wind will come to blow away.

Unlike them, I am consumed at your hearth's heat
and refined to the precious metal that will last
forever. The worthless goods of the world I cast
out or, better, I lay them at your feet.

You are my empire, world, my universe
which, without you, is nothing, and I am worse
than nothing, negative space, a mere void.

A death from the tortures of my love for you
is better than any life given over to
such luxuries as can never be enjoyed.

Les vents grondaient en l'air, les plus sombres nuages
Nous dérobaient le jour pêle-mêle entassés,
Les abîmes d'enfer étaient au ciel poussés,
La mer s'enflait de monts, et le monde d'orages:

Quand je vis qu'un oiseau délaissant nos rivages
S'envole au beau milieu de ses flots courroucés,
Y pose de son nid les fétus ramassés
Et rapaise soudain ses écumeuses rages.

L'amour m'en fit autant, et comme un Alcyon,
L'autre jour se logea dedans ma passion
Et combla de bonheur mon âme infortunée.

Après le trouble, enfin, il me donna la paix:
Mais le calme de mer n'est qu'une fois l'année,
Et celui de mon âme y sera pour jamais.

## XXVI

The winds howled and a mountain range of cloud
loomed overhead to darken the daylight sky
as black as a night in hell, and the sea ran high,
driven to madness by that keening, loud

and endless, but then I saw a small bird flutter
into that maelstrom, in her beak a straw
for her floating nest, and I observed in awe
as the storm abated suddenly to utter

halcyon calm. So my love died in me
to happiness and the peace of a glassy sea
on which my spirit has settled. My mind is clear;

my faith has been rewarded; for all my pain
there is a joy that I know shall obtain
forever, though at sea it is one day a year.

*Sonnets de la mort*
Sonnets on Death

Mortels, qui des mortels avez pris votre vie,
Vie qui meurt encor dans le tombeau du Corps,
Vous qui ramoncelez vos trésors, des trésors
De ceux dont par la mort la vie fut ravie:

Vous qui voyant de morts leur mort entresuivie,
N'avez point de maisons que les maisons des morts,
Et ne sentez pourtant de la mort un remords,
D'où vient qu'au souvenir son souvenir s'oublie?

Est-ce que votre vie adorant ses douceurs
Déteste des pensers de la mort les horreurs,
Et ne puisse envier une contraire envie?

Mortels, chacun accuse, et j'excuse le tort
Qu'on forge en votre oubli. Un oubli d'une mort
Vous monstre un souvenir d'une éternelle vie.

» » » I

Mortals who from mortals received the spark
of life that ends in the body's tomb, you run
after the orts of those who have been undone
by death, ravished and dragged down to the dark. . . .

We never mind: but that is the death of the dead—
that we do not remember them or feel remorse.
We have our own lives to lead, of course,
and are better occupied with pleasure than dread.

Death can wait, and, patiently, it does,
whether we dwell on it or not. It has
seen before how the timid, vain, or clever

contrive to deny to themselves the obvious truth:
that they have forgotten the days of their own youth
and are in a decline that cannot go on forever.

Mais si faut-il mourir! et la vie orgueilleuse,
Qui brave de la mort, sentira ses fureurs;
Les Soleils hâleront ces journalières fleurs,
Et le temps crèvera cette ampoule venteuse.

Ce beau flambeau qui lance une flamme fumeuse,
Sur le vert de la cire éteindra ses ardeurs;
L'huile de ce Tableau ternira ses couleurs,
Et ses flots se rompront à la rive écumeuse.

J'ai vu ces clairs éclairs passer devant mes yeux,
Et le tonnerre encor qui gronde dans les Cîeux.
Ou d'une ou d'autre part éclatera l'orage.

J'ai vu fondre la neige et ces torrents tarir,
Ces lions rugissants, je les ai vus sans rage.
Vivez, hommes, vivez, mais si faut-il mourir.

In the face of death, how is it that life can be
proud? That horror should put it to shame. A flower
blossoms at dawn; by noon sun in its power
has burned it to a husk. The torch we see

blazing at dinner will gutter out, and the paint
on the picture on the wall will craze and fade
to something less than what the artist made,
a memory of itself we watch grow faint.

The lightning flash and thunder fade away.
December's drifts will disappear by May
in freshets that, in summer, themselves, run dry.

This energy, these marvels on every side
command like the roars of lions in their pride,
so full of life because they will one day die.

Ha! que j'en vois bien peu songer à cette mort
Et si chacun la cerche aux dangers de la guerre!
Tantôt dessus la Mer, tantôt dessus la Terre,
Mais las! dans son oubli tout le monde s'endort.

De la Mer, on s'attend à resurgir au Port,
Sur la Terre, aux effrois dont l'ennemi s'atterre:
Bref, chacun pense à vivre, et ce vaisseau de verre
S'estime être un rocher bien solide et bien fort.

Je vois ces vermisseaux bâtir dedans leurs plaines
Les monts de leurs desseins, dont les cimes humaines
Semblent presque égaler leurs coeurs ambitieux.

Géants, où poussez-vous ces beaux amas de poudre?
Vous les amoncelez? Vous les verrez dissoudre:
Ils montent de la Terre? Ils tomberont des Cieux.

» » » III

How few I see who think of dying, save
on battlefields, which one can try to evade
or avoid, or boarding ships, when one is afraid
of the vastness of the sea that he must brave,

leaving terra firma—except that ground
is quicksand. We forget that death is near
always and everywhere and that our fear
is justified. Our vessels are unsound.

Those men of affairs who hurry through the town
are blind as the worms to which time will bring down
their hopes, their golden dreams. Their labors all

must crumble, turn to dust, and blow away.
We work, we scheme, we bully, or we pray
and try to soar toward heaven, but we fall.

Pour qui tant de trauvaux? pour vous? de qui l'haleine
Pantelle en la poitrine et traîne sa langueur?
Vos desseins sont bien loin du bout de leur vigueur
Et vous êtes bien près du bout de votre peine.

Je vous accorde encore une emprise certaine,
Qui de soi court du Temps l'incertaine rigueur;
Si perdrez-vous enfin ce fruit et ce labeur:
Le Mont est foudroyé plus souvent que la plaine.

Ces Sceptres enviés, ces Trésors débattus,
Champ superbe du camp de vos fières vertus,
Sont de l'avare mort le débat et l'envie.

Mais pourquoi ce souci? mais pourquoi cet effort?
Savez-vous bien que c'est le train de cette vie?
La fuite de la Vie, et la course à la Mort.

All these travails! For whom? For you, whose breath
flutters within your chest and stops and then
starts up again? You plan great projects when
that little time you have before your death

diminishes by the day and hour. You
apply yourself with ever greater zeal
to schemes that lose their purpose and appeal
through life's decay. What else is there to do?

But look to the mountaintop where lighting likes
to dance. (On the plain below it seldom strikes.)
Death's envious eye is on your trophy case:

your many sterling virtues are arrayed
and all your proud achievements are displayed
that will be his when you have run your race.

Hélas! contez vos jours: les jours qui sont passés
Sont déjà morts pour vous, ceux qui viennent encore
Mourront tous sur le point de leur naissante Aurore,
Et moitié de la vie est moitié du décès.

Ces désirs orgueilleux pêle-mêle entassés,
Ce coeur outrecuidé que votre bras implore,
Cet indomptable bras que votre coeur adore,
La Mort les met en gêne, et leur fait le procès.

Mille flots, mille écueils, font tête à votre route,
Vous rompez à travers, mais à la fin, sans doute,
Vous serez le butin des écueils, et des flots,

Une heure vous attend, un moment vous épie,
Bourreaux dénaturés de votre propre vie,
Qui vit avec la peine, et meurt sans le repos.

»»» V

Alas, your days are numbered: those that have past
are dead; and in the others still to come
dawn will break broken and suffering from
mortality's shadow that on all time is cast.

Your arrogant desire to amass
strange trophies and the passionate heart you reach
to embrace, death snatches away, as if to teach
your dullard soul the basics of his class.

Obstacles, hazards, shoals, chicanes impede
the way you blunder through; your lust and greed
are your blind guides, and you are ruined, wrecked.

Your hour awaits: its moments are standing by,
the judges who try and sentence you to die
in torment still. What else did you expect?

Tout le monde se plaint de la cruelle envie
Que la nature porte aux longueurs de nos jours
Hommes, vous vous trompez, ils ne sont pas trop courts
Si vous vous mesurez au pied de votre vie.

Mais quoi? je n'entends point quelqu'un de vous qui dit:
Je me veux dépêtrer de ces fâcheux détours,
Il faut que je revole à ces plus beaux séjours,
Ou séjourne des Temps l'entresuite infinie.

Beaux séjours, loin de l'oeil, près de l'entendement,
Au prix de qui ce Temps ne monte qu'un moment,
Au prix de qui le jour est un ombrage sombre,

Vous êtes mon désir: et ce jour, et ce Temps,
Où le Monde s'aveugle et prend son passetemps,
Ne me seront jamais qu'un moment et qu'une Ombre.

Everyone complains how Nature is
so covetous of our drawn-out days of leisure.
We fool ourselves: these stretches without measure
prove finite after all, parentheses

in life's terse sentences. A man will say
he is impatient for the time to pass,
but I do not understand. Suppose he has
appointments in that mansion far away:

there time is of no moment, and desire,
fulfilled at once, leaves nothing to require.
Wanting nothing, one has it, so to speak.

This lower world of shifting shadows turns
in retrospect attractive, and one learns
one's lesson: that desire is what we seek.

Tandis que dedans l'air un autre air je respire,
Et qu'à l'envi du feu j'allume mon désir,
Que j'enfle contre l'eau les eaux de mon plaisir,
Et que me colle à Terre un importun martyre,

Cet air toujours m'anime, et le désir m'attire,
Je recherche à monceaux les plaisirs à choisir,
Mon martyre élevé me vient encor saisir,
Et de tous mes travaux le dernier est le pire.

A la fin je me trouve en un étrange émoi,
Car ces divers effets ne sont que contre moi:
C'est mourir que de vivre en cette peine extrême.

Voilà comme la vie à l'abandon s'épart:
Chaque part de ce Monde en emporte sa part,
Et la moindre à la fin est celle de nous-mêmes.

# »»» VII

Here in this air, I breathe a rarer air
as my soul ignites with another finer fire.
In this ebb tide, I ride a flood of desire
but the earth will not release me from its snare.

I raise my eyes as I, myself, would rise
to float upon that ether for which I yearn,
but sensual pleasures beckon and I burn
in martyrdom (except that a martyr dies).

It is a war in which both sides must lose,
and I am ruined because I cannot choose
this world or that wholeheartedly. Instead,

I temporize, uncertain and afraid,
condemned to exist in a limbo I have made,
a mortal, neither truly alive nor dead.

Voulez-vous voir ce trait qui si raide s'élance
Dedans l'air qu'il poursuit au partir de la main?
Il monte, il monte, il perd: mais hélas! tout soudain
Il retombe, il retombe, et perd sa violence.

C'est le train de nos jours, c'est cette outrecuidance
Que ces Monstres de Terre allaittent de leur sein,
Qui baise ores des monts le sommet plus hautain,
Ores sur les rochers de ces vallons s'offense.

Voire, ce sont nos jours: quand tu seras monté
A ce point de hauteur, à ce point arrêté
Qui ne se peut forcer, il te faudra descendre.

Le trait est empenné, l'air qu'il va poursuivant
C'est le champ de l'orage: hé! commence d'apprendre
Que ta vie est de Plume, et le monde de Vent.

Observe, if you would, this arrow rising high,
almost straight up and, apparently, unaware
of parabolas. You realize that somewhere
is an apogee, where it must fall from the sky.

This is our days' trajectory, too, their stern
program we cannot escape: no matter how
we scramble up the face of the mountain now,
that cold peak looms from which we must return.

We pretend it is not so, for who could bear
the dismal truth? An arrow flies through the air
decked out with pretty feathers to guide its force,

and it seems at home in the sky. But it will stop
its climb to yield to gravity's sway and drop.
So runs our lives' inevitable course.

Qui sont, qui sont ceux là, dont le coeur idolâtre
Se jette aux pieds du Monde, et flatte ses honneurs?
Et qui sont ces Valets, et qui sont ces Seigneurs?
Et ces âmes d'Ebène, et ces faces d'Albâtre?

Ces masques déguisés, dont la troupe folâtre
S'amuse à caresser je ne sais quels donneurs
De fumées de Court, et ces entrepreneurs
De vaincre encor le Ciel qu'ils ne peuvent combattre?

Qui sont ces louvoyeurs qui s'éloignent du Port?
Hommagers à la Vie, et félons à la Mort,
Dont l'étoile est leur Bien, le vent leur Fantaisie?

Je vogue en même mer, et craindrais de périr
Si ce n'est que je sais que cette même vie
N'est rien que le fanal qui me guide au mourir.

Who are they, then, those idol worshipers who
so love the world and its honors and rewards
that they become its servants more than its lords
and lose or deform their souls by what they do?

These maskers at a costume ball pretend
to one another that they are fooled, although
they recognize beneath each domino
the acquaintance whom they cannot call a friend.

Who are these privateers who tack and trim
guided by their ambition and their whim?
Can they ignore that beacon light I see

by which we all must set a course? I run
downwind, however I steer, and when I'm done,
I'll make fast in that berth death keeps for me.

Mais si mon faible corps (qui comme l'eau s'écoule
Et s'affermit encor plus longtemps qu'un plus fort)
S'avance à tous moments vers le seuil de la mort,
Et que mal dessus mal dans le tombeau me roule,

Pourquoi tiendrai-je raide à ce vent qui saboule
Le Sablon de mes jours d'un invincible effort?
Faut-il pas réveiller cette Ame qui s'endort,
De peur qu'avec le corps la Tempête la foule?

Laisse dormir ce corps, mon Ame, et quant à toi
Veille, veille et te tiens alerte à tout effroi,
Garde que ce Larron ne te trouve endormie:

Le point de sa venue est pour nous incertain,
Mais, mon Ame, il suffit que cet Auteur de Vie
Nous cache bien son temps, mais non pas son dessein.

»»» X

My feeble body deteriorates: it flows
downhill as surely as water does to seek
its lowest level. I feel myself grow weak
approaching death's threshold. Meanwhile, my woes

burden me further. Grief upon grief I bear.
Suppose a desert wind that drifts the sand
to cover a house, a town. . . . Can I withstand
such overwhelming force as I find there?

Then let it go, my soul, for you can live
without it! Look to your own affairs, and give
your thought to what must come. On this reflect:

the Author of the Book of Life is kind
and may conceal the time, but we're not blind
to his design: we know what to expect.

Et quel bien de la Mort? où la vermine ronge
Tous ces nerfs, tous ces os; où l'Ame se départ
De cette orde charogne, et se tient à l'écart,
Et laisse un souvenir de nous comme d'un songe?

Ce corps, qui dans la vie en ses grandeurs se plonge,
Si soudain dans la mort étouffera sa part,
Et sera ce beau Nom, qui tant partout s'épart,
Borné de vanité, couronné de mensonge.

A quoi cette Ame, hélas! et ce corps désunis?
Du commerce du monde hors du monde bannis?
A quoi ces noeuds si beaux que le Trépas délie?

Pour vivre au Ciel il faut mourir plutôt ici:
Ce n'en est pas pourtant le sentier raccourci,
Mais quoi? nous n'avons plus ni d'Hénoch ni d'Elie.

And why should Death be proud, if vermin teem
over our bones and delicate nerves and the Soul
flees this loathsome carrion (its goal
is elsewhere than this shadow of a dream)?

The body that in life pursued its lust
and hunger is refined to a name and then
chewed in the mouths of envious lying men,
its hope of fame corrupted to disgust.

Riven apart, the soul and body long
for one another and the world, the strong
bonds that held them having come apart,

as Heaven requires. Each one who dies on earth
must leave a corpse below for his rebirth—
save Enoch, or Elijah in his cart.

## »»» XII

Tout s'enfle contre moi, tout m'assaut, tout me tente,
Et le Monde et la Chair, et l'Ange révolté,
Dont l'onde, dont l'effort, dont le charme inventé
Et m'abîme, Seigneur, et m'ébranle, et m'enchante.

Quelle nef, quel appui, quelle oreille dormante,
Sans péril, sans tomber, et sans être enchanté,
Me donras-tu? Ton Temple où vit la Sainteté,
Ton invincible main, et ta voix si constante?

Et quoi? Mon Dieu, je sens combattre maintes fois
Encor avec ton Temple, et ta main, et ta voix,
Cet Ange révolté, cette Chair, et ce Monde.

Mais ton Temple pourtant, ta main, ta voix sera
La nef, l'appui, l'oreille, où ce charme perdra,
Où mourra cet effort, où se perdra cette onde.

## »»» XII

I am besieged and undermined, undone:
the World, the Flesh, and the Fallen Angel conspire
to ruin me, exploiting my desire. . . .
Help me, O Lord! Seize me before I'm gone.

Send me a sign, a ship, a prop, relief
from some unexpected quarter. Lead me to
your sanctuary and heal me. See me through
this valley. Do not let me come to grief.

Your steady hand, your voice, your temple's door . . .
these are my only hope, and I implore
your mercy. Fend the Devil off and save

a desperate soul. Without that prop, that barque,
that sign I need and pray for in the dark,
I must go under, drowned by the next wave.

## » Bibliographic Note

There is a useful biography, *Vie de Jean de Sponde,* by Alan Boase
(Geneva: Librairie Droz, 1977), who is also the editor of Sponde's
*Oeuvres littéraires* (Geneva: Librairie Droz, 1978). Sabine Lar-
don has written what is surely the best book-length considera-
tion of Sponde's work, *L'écriture de la méditation chez Jean de
Sponde* (Paris: Honoré Champion, 1998). Lardon also has an
edition of Sponde's *Méditations sur les pseaumes* (Paris: Honoré
Champion, 1996), which offers an extensive bibliography. The
other translations of Sponde's *Sonnets of Love and Death* into
English are those of G. F. Cunningham (Edinburgh: Olivier and
Boyd, 1964) and of Robert Nugent (Painesville, Ohio: Lake Erie
College Studies, 1962).

*About the Author*

Jean de Sponde, a French poet, translator, humanist, jurist, and Hellenist, was born in 1557. His translation of Homer, *Homeri poemarum versio latina,* was used by George Chapman, and he also published a scholarly edition of *La Logique d'Aristotle.* After leading a reckless life at the court of Henry IV, Sponde converted to Catholicism. He died destitute in Bordeaux, France, in 1595.

> I just write as I like, carelessly, and get through
> with it. . . . I don't have any limitation of time
> and place for my writing. I even allow people to
> interfere. . . . My friends know that I usually sit
> and write at the dining table in the sitting room
> while my family watches TV. My son comes
> every now and then, asking me questions about
> math. I explain to him, then go on with my
> writing. . . . To me writing has become a natural
> way of life. I have no set goals, but only an
> impulse from inside and endless desire.

So far this method has yielded the stories collected
here, two novellas, and, most recently, a novel of
200,000 Chinese characters (*The Performance of Break-
Through*), which she has called "a peak in my writing,"
saying that "it records my whole world outlook and
my opinions about love. What's more," she continues,
"the technique of presentation is unique. . . . It is very
abstract, very obscure — full of the power to repel
readers!"

The stories gathered in the present volume are
arranged to lead the reader into Can Xue's fictional
world, beginning with works that come as close as she
probably ever will to recognizable narrative realism
and proceeding toward free flights of primary pro-
cesses — fantasy, dream, nightmare. At times her sto-
ries can be as acerbically funny as Lu Xun's *The True
Story of Ah Q* or as terrifying as his "Diary of a Mad-
man." Each of the shorter works is a drama of conflict,
an agon, most often embedded in a pervasive dark-
ness, but sometimes penetrated by a blaze of light, at
other times bathed in a soft mist. The rhythms and

tones of her scenes evoke the reader's emotions, the seeming non sequiturs and sudden transformations disrupt the easy expectations of logical thought. And all of this is wrapped in Can Xue's particular powers — the bitter humor, the lyrical flights, the philosophical probings — that challenge stony reality, recreating it while seeking channels of escape and transcendence.

Those who accept the difficulties of Can Xue's work will find themselves, finally, in a realm ("paradise," she calls it in her memoir) where understanding itself becomes a creative enterprise, less restricted to the literal or denotative surface of the work and more engaged with the tonalities, the metamorphic structures, and the plastic sense inherent to the creative as opposed to the journalistic arts.

The transformative powers of Can Xue's imagination are particularly evident in the last several stories in this volume, especially in the title piece, "Dialogues in Paradise." The central elements of the five sections of this story are imbued with the power of myth. The narrator sees herself being "as ancient as this savage place" and experiences her life "stretching in one direction, infinitely." On one side of her stands a male figure who serves as teacher, advisor, guardian, lover, and, in section four, seducer in a deadly game; on the other side, a third figure — shadowy and elusive, sometimes male, sometimes female — who may or may not pose a real threat to her.

The narrative is woven of images of drifting, floating, flying, constant seeking with no clear goal. The subject of the story seems to be process itself — the

ongoing flow of things beyond any stabilized reality —
rising to tension in the fourth section:

> I have been searching. I may find something
> again. (This is a vast world.) It is an unbreakable
> wicked circle. Evil spirits rise in the profound
> darkness, hairy plants swell rapidly. Does the
> wolf in the iron cage run day and night in its
> narrow world?

The narrow world of the wolf's iron cage rhymes
with other settings in Can Xue's stories: locked huts,
run-down temples, crowded houses, dark rooms — all
places where, as the narrator in "Skylight" says, "when
night comes, we sneak in panic . . . like rats looking
for the darkest and remotest place." Ultimately, the
narrow space is the mind itself, where all the external
tensions of parent and child, husband and wife, com-
munity and individual have been internalized. Soci-
ology becomes pathology, perception drifts into
hallucination and nightmare, the whole bringing her
narrators, as she says in "Dialogues," to "face the hor-
rifying abyss."

Can Xue's remarks on her creative ideals range be-
tween metaphorical polarities: the deepening, the
probing of the inner mind, and the flight of fantasy,
the act of magical transformation. Unlike the realist's,
her art, in its freest moments, arises from the shifting
processes of exploration rather than the solid ground
of the given — narration as improvisation rather than
retelling, the sentence that leads rather than follows,
lifting the mind to new wonders rather than settling

it into old familiarities or predictabilities, the art of dream and truth in an uncertain time.

The stories offered here are eloquent in a way that the West associates with both the modern and the ancient — the dark oracles of Aeschylus and Sophocles, the paranoid mystery of Kafka, the moving stream of Woolf. Can Xue's work renews our consciousness of the long tradition of the irrational in our own literature, where dream and reality are no longer separate realms but rather constitute one territory, its borders open, the passage back and forth barely discernible.

Can Xue has staked out territory explored by none of her contemporaries in China. Her stories transcend the local without losing the "bite" of the quotidian. She opens up the Chinese character while also revealing qualities which can everywhere be recognized as profoundly human. In doing so, she has offered Chinese fiction a provocative challenge, and a direction for new growth.

# Notes

1. Remarks attributed to Can Xue are drawn from letters written to Ronald Janssen between March 1986 and November 1987.

2. The quotations in this paragraph are drawn from letters to Ronald Janssen from correspondents who wish to remain anonymous. They also appear in Janssen, "Intellectuals in Modern and Contemporary China," *Bulletin of Concerned Asian Scholars* 20:1 (January–March 1988), 62.

3. Quoted in Moss Roberts, ed. and trans., *Chinese Fairy Tales and Fantasies* (New York: Pantheon Books, 1979), 19. Pinyin spelling of Zhuangzi supplied by Ronald Janssen.